CROSSING HIGHER GROUND

POETRY FROM THE MOUNTAINTOPS

RICK VAN DE POLL

Illustrated by
ARIANNA RELANDER

OWL FEATHER PRESS, LLC

Crossing Higher Ground:
Poetry from the Mountaintops

ISBN: 978-0-9994808-2-3

Published by Owl Feather Press, LLC
Illustrated by Arianna Relander
Formatted by Spirit Paw Press, LLC

To all people who have chosen to make mountain living a regular part of their life,

and

To all organisms who, by way of their incredible adaptation, do not need to make a choice

CONTENTS

FOREWORD

These are the stories that mountains tell. For people have been coming to mountains for centuries, honoring their gods, communing with spirits, escaping enemies, hunting food, seeking shelter, testing their resolve, and tempting fate. Ultimately, one stands alone on the mountain of life, facing oneself. If one believes that 'the endurant liveth forever,' then the mountain reminds us that even this adage in untrue. Humans have walked in the valleys that were mountains once and will be mountains again. If geologic time casts a glance back upon what was once there, then our blink-of-the-eye time on Earth suggests that mountains have a great many more stories to tell.

Mountains then, become our teachers. They force us to look up at the lofty heights and to the heavens beyond. They remind us of the immutable force of gravity and the perils of taking such a force for granted. They bear the secrets of continents in their bones, yet give up those secrets slowly, carefully, and only to the intentional, inquisitive eye. Their accounting of the passage of time bears witness to every chapter of Earth's history, and as such forces us to reflect upon the chapter that we as a species are living in today.

INTRODUCTION

The view from a mountaintop is perfectly unique. No other vantage point in a given area (short of, say, the Empire State Building), can offer such perspective. The freshness of the air, the vastness of the horizon that surrounds, and the infinite silence that attends these high points offers a sense of wonder and awe. The world falls away from beneath your feet and for a moment, the flight of birds comes easily to mind.

This is the context in which I have written my second book of poetry. It was inspired by the countless mountaintops I have witnessed as well as the trials and tribulations of getting there. Fifty years of wandering has yielded many a lesson from the ascent of high peaks and brought with it a perspective on humankind that would otherwise be missing from my life.

Thrice I have survived what should have been my end. For gravity has a way of teaching most of us climbers the cost of making a mistake. For my part, I have been beset with greater humility each time I survived, only to wonder what path was yet in store from my future wanderings. While in service to the planet, humanity, and all wild things, I have typically not had to wonder very long.

For there is without a doubt a great need to understand our place in the world and to be of service to it.

Humanity stands at the brink of its own survival. For some, it's a numbers game—7 billion people and counting; nearly 1 million cases of Covid-19 and counting; 410 parts per million CO_2 and counting; 2.2 degrees Celsius higher and counting. For others, it's a wait-and-see game—invest in 'smart money;' don't rock the boat at your job; keep a low profile. For others still it's a wild ride—to the North Pole, to the top of Everest, to the bottom of the Mariana Trench, or perhaps even to Mars.

Yet this planet is still worth saving. Why throw it all away because society is short-sighted, or irresponsible about our impacts on the Earth, or a little too greedy to care enough to change our traditions, to change our life styles, to change the way we consume things?

What we need is better perspective.

While it may not require climbing to the highest of mountains to gain such a perspective, it has seemed to help me on my path. I have learned great things from both the places I have been and the people who have helped me get there. With any luck, some of these lessons will come through in this collection of poems and short essays. With even greater luck, some of these lessons will be beneficial to those of my readers who have not yet climbed to a higher ground to gain such a new perspective.

With the greatest respect for all of the mountain people who have come before me, and those who will follow, as well as the valley people who have aided me along the way, I owe you all a debt of gratitude for accepting me into the echelon of 'survivalists.' It seems that we are, after all, the ones who will be able to help usher in a new age for our grandchildren's grandchildren.

Rick Van de Poll

Sandwich, NH

July 2020

https://rickvandepoll.com

PART I
THE APPROACH

THE APPROACH

1

MOUNTAINS SO HIGH

At first, I can only imagine a tiny speck of
  purple in the distance,
Then it becomes blue,
And finally green, black and white as it grows
  closer upon my approach.
The loftiness is hidden as it always is in the
  valley of my beginning.
Each peak seems to be taller in my mind.
Over and over again I go over the route,
Imagining every traverse, every arrête, every
  bergshrund, the final cone.
I can feel the kick-steps, one by one, going on
  forever,
Soft snow, then crampon tip ice, then soft
  again.
Kicking the clumps off on some rock,
Taking care not to loosen another landslide.

I can see it now, those ever so familiar snowy
  slopes,
How will they be today? Foul and unforgiving,
Or kind and yielding?
My wishes become prayers of thanks and
  providence,
As if I can actually speak to the Mountain, and
  it to me,
Listening for the right to pass,
A sign, an omen of good fortune.
But none has come today, either bad or good.
Today I must keep my wits about me,
And pay attention to every step!

THE APPROACH.

Car now parked, I disembark.
I pack carefully, heavy enough to survive on,
  but light to enough to be quick.
Agility and endurance must come today in
  equal measure.
The pack straps feels taut as I stretch out on
  the first leg,
Fending off the coolness of dawn with a steady,
  'get there' pace.
The trail winds upwards, gentle at first, and
  then more steeply,
I push first break to the limit of thirst,
The hard work still lies ahead.
A gulp and a swallow, and my muscles are

*already re-hydrating for what will be a
    long, slow climb.*
I pass the first gate.
*It isn't as visible as it often is, but it's there
    nonetheless.*
*An old subalpine fir has supined its branches
    upon the ground,*
Guarding the path with its outstretched arms.
*It beckons, I give thanks, lay tobacco, and
    move on.*
*The way is gentler now, accepting me forward,
    onward, and up.*
*Trees thin out, the overwhelming scent of
    glacier lilies has quickened my pace,*
*I would run were it not a race against what lies
    ahead.*
*The vision of distant peaks, valleys, and ocean
    bring me home once more,*
I have come again to even the score.

THE ASCENT.

*The trail has left me now, long ago left to the
    feet of the pathtakers,*
*Rock and snow stand high above me as I take
    my first look at the climb.*
*The route still looks doable – a traverse on
    scree, a direct ascent up the snow chute,*
*Tracking the upper edge of avalanche alders as
    I call them,*

*A 500 meter scramble up a rocky arête, and on
to the upper glacier field.*
So far so good.
*The loose talus brings sweat to my forehead as
I take two steps for every step gained.*
Pika whistles blast out from across the valley,
*An undersized denizen that polices my every
move.*
*If I could only pass unnoticed I think to
myself,*
*A foolish thought for one so gigantic, armed
with vibram and ice axe!*
*Alpine flowers dance beneath my feet, like so
many sirens*
*Ushering me to slowness, casting an ethereal
drowsiness upon my inquisitive brain,*
*But onward I must go! Tarry not, or be the
midnight fool once again!*
*(Dare I repeat what Mount Constance
taught me?)*
*The steep snow slope anchors my mind, well
away from such distraction,*
Kick, breath, kick, breath, kick, breath,
*The altitude has sharpened my focus, and
forced me into mechanical movement,*
*A quiet meditation of respect for the inevitable
pull of gravity upon this Earth.*
*Pitch two has gone well, the ice axe handle
feels strong in my hand.*
The rock face draws near.
*That cavalcade of grayish-brown is now a series
of broken bands of rock,*

*A veritable tapestry of tepid umber brown and
    blackish hues,*
*Streaked with cinnamon slides and milky
    swirls,*
A magmatic mud pie with vanilla frosting.
(God am I hungry!)
The scramble is now in hand,
*On mountain goat fours I work my way up the
    arête,*
*Barely touching the rock as it taunts with
    daggers and knives,*
And ascend the final pitch to the second gate.
*Two large boulders frame an impossibly vast
    ice field,*
*Stretching out before me like a velvet carpet in
    the sun,*
Shimmering hot, I step into the heat.

THE TRAVERSE.

The icy blanket unfolds before me,
*At first drawn up like a warm shawl upon the
    cirque,*
*Then broken, aching, revealing age lines
    remarkably old,*
*Yawning crevasses yearn to swallow my steps as
    I pick my way,*
Snow bridges firm in the morning sun,
Unpredictable by afternoon's light,
*Everywhere the sound of water dripping deep
    into the fathoms,*

I trudge on.
It seems like miles have passed now with corn
   snow underfoot,
Slipping with every step,
Like so many dreams of trying to run from
   danger,
But going nowhere,
Mired in a slow-motion ascent that approaches
   glacial velocity.
Somewhere above me a cracked cornice let
   loose a once-frozen rock,
Freed by the mid-morning sun,
Careening downslope at an incredible speed in
   my direction,
A quick dodge and I avert the threat,
And watch as it takes flight at the next
   crevasse,
Smashing into the sidewall,
Delivering ice and broken rock deep into the
   cavern,
Echoes resounding beneath at unknowable
   depths.
I climb on.
The snow cups have deepened,
Casting an ethereal pinkish glow upon the
   upper edge,
I bend down and scoop up a handful,
Clean off debris and hungry snow spiders,
And taste the watermelon ice,
An algal elixir that freshens my step.
Cutting into the shaded side of each cup,
I ascend slowly towards the gaping maw ahead,

A bergshrund so wide I'm forced to cut a snow
    anchor,
And body rappel down into its very throat,
Only to expel myself with convulsive force
    over scree and rock,
Breathing hard,
Glad to be out of dark spaces where nothing
    ever good comes of a climber there.

THE SUMMIT CONE.

Long have I looked upon the pinnacle of this
    climb.
The sight of it has been etched into my
    memory for as long as I can remember.
Like the last time, my approach has been from
    the east,
But the slant terraces curve around to the west.
No one can see what's on the west.
Like the dark side of the moon,
The hidden face of the cone remains unknown,
Except to those who have ventured forth,
Most never to be heard from again.
The east side captures the breadth of the upper
    snowfield,
The upper apex of which has favorably
    provided access to the most direct face.
Solo now, unlike the last time where I top-lead
    the east face route,
I choose mystery.
The west beckons,

Like so many bears in winter,
Who go to sleep trusting there will be spring.
I must learn to trust my instincts as well, and
the west is calling.
The first ramp delivers me to the southeast
ridge,
And a sheer drop beyond.
Blocked, I look up.
There, high above, a pair of boulders await,
I pitch up easily and reach the third gate.
Before me lies a path, a very old path, that
leads to the summit.
But to get there I must navigate an exposed
ledge, roughly 200 meters high.
Resting now in the protective folds of this final
doorway,
I cast about my gaze, my thoughts, my
wondering.
Is this it? My final view? My last recollection of
the montane West,
My 'Ricci Serafino' moment like in the Italian
Alps?
I trust it will not be,
I trust my feet, my arms, my legs, my
choices,
I trust my teachers, all of those before me, who
have imparted in me skill,
I trust my knowledge of loose rock and hard
rock, and the wisdom of knowing the
difference,
I trust my balance, and the ways of my
mountain goat friends,

*I trust that the path will indeed lead to the
      summit,
And more importantly,
That it will lead me back,
I trust.
I affix axe to pack, take a slug of water, and
      tighten straps.
The first step loosens some small rock, and I
      catch myself up.
Caution, now, caution.
The second and third go smoothly and
      carefully, gradually, I climb upwards.
A short pitch to a crack, a traverse to a
      chimney and slowly inching up to the next
      face.
Two lengths up, and there it is.
The rate determining step.
There is always a rate-determining step.
Like some pesky chemical reaction,
These have been the bane of my climbing
      existence:
The point at which I can either proceed with
      extreme danger, or turn around.
These are the points that insurance adjusters
      shy away from, earth quake engineers
      abhor, coastal strand developers don't talk
      about.
You either do it, take the risk, and face the
      consequences, or you give up.
Life is so very much like that in every way.
At what point do we turn around and give in
      to the fear of certain death?*

It's different for everyone.
For me perhaps, (since I tend to find some
kind of hard protection at the top of such
pitches I insist on climbing), it's a little
later than for most.
The severity of the pitch and the amount of
exposure forces me to consider the options.
Downclimb? Not advisable. Lateral traverse?
Worse.
Today, for me, it's just another chemical
reaction – a rate-determining step.
I choose the rate by determining my step.
I grow small in my focus and rivet my energies
towards the rock.
I maintain control, control every move, move
with the rock, and let the rock move me.
Not unlike some deep meditation I have
experienced, I lose track of time.
In seconds (minutes?) I am above the rate-
determining step, into the safety of another
chimney, and emerge onto the final path.
There it lies before me, the final ascent to the
summit rocks.
It's a walk up.
I breathe deep, give thanks, and kneel into the
mountain once again,
Thankful I have been give the grace to find my
summit waiting for me at last.

～

This poem is a compendium of all of the major climbs I have completed. It includes four typical elements of every climb–the approach, the climb or ascent, the traverse, and the summit cone. The approach represents a rapid stage of growing and learning about the mountain, the consideration of how to ascend the mountain, and the recognition of one's own physical limitations. The climb or ascent engages the skills and endurance of the climber, requires the greatest attention, and focuses the climber on the chosen route. The traverse is often a less steep, apparently easier portion that can make one feel like they're on 'cruise control,' yet it is usually beset with pitfalls and dangers that are unforeseen, and can bring about an unwitting death or tragedy. The end of the traverse often includes the 'rate determining step,' a critical point that requires the firmest resolve of the climber, the one where a single mistake means death, and where often a greater wisdom finds the climber turning back. Once past this point, the traverse ends easily and is usually followed by the final ascent of the summit. Depending on the route chosen, the summit cone is usually less technical and ends with a safe and rewarding walk-up to the top. Each stage typically marks time by "gates," which represent symbolic portals between each of the basic elements. These can be obvious, like the face of a cliff, or subtle, like a passageway between two boulders or saracs.

2

BACK TO BASICS

I breathe
And the breath of my ancestors is within me
I feel
And the heart of all people beats again
I listen
And the echo of memory resounds within
I see
And the whole world is watching through my
*   eyes,*
That which is separate
Is naught
But a reflection of my own design,
I walk now with the Earth becoming my
*   mind.*
Where do I begin?

~

C limbing a mountain puts one in touch with the basic rhythms of life – breath, heartbeat, hearing, vision, sensation. Understanding the connection between these aspects of self and the 'other' – in this case, the mountain, can inspire an understanding of the connection between self and the peopled past, especially all of those who have walked on the same mountain journey you are embarking upon. Understanding those connections can deepen the meaning of the climb as it so very often has for me when beginning the approach.

3

THE ASCENT

A path forward becomes me,
To the Left? To the Right? I know not.
Forward then it is through this Gordian knot,
I'm climbing now,
Climbing through the wilderness of my mind,
Unfamiliar places not yet lost to humankind,
Not sure how I got here,
But somehow I don't mind,
For here is a path reminiscent of a long ago
*   time,*
When journeying was an art and not a trifling
*   crime.*

~

I write this poem to highlight the symbolism of choosing a particular path, which quite literally can make all the difference in one's life. Going left or going right in a single step can lead a person in a completely different direction with different life path partners, different avocations, different physical and emotional trials, and different opportunities to live a fulfilling life. This poem also honors the Golden Age of journeying where one's life path was understood to be more important than all of the wealth & riches, political influence, and opulent possession of goods a single person could muster.

4

A WISH

I wait, and I watch,
And I wait a little more
I long for the keys to open the door,
A wild world awaits and I've patience no more,
Yet I am but a child in the woods,
Crawling on all fours,
Feeling blind and alone, and lost evermore.
There must be a path,
I believe there must be,
That once I have taken it
Will set my soul free,
For long have I spoken to my animal kin,
And rejected the myth of Original Sin,
And with practice I have learned to listen
     again,
And find peace among those who can see me
     within,

For in a world without hate, or fear-based
　　dominion,
The wild ones will come to us and welcome
　　us in.

～

The passage intends to honor the presence of mind of all wild things. Many times I have imagined what it would be like to be a wolf or bear or moose and live among kin where choices are largely driven by heredity and biology. Such biology, however, prescribes choices that are often made on the basis of cues that are all but imperceptible to humans. What would be like to think and act like an elephant, or an orangutan, or a polar bear, or a honey bee? What would the world be like without a top predator that mostly disrespects all other life and seeks only to hold dominion over all other living things including its own species?

5

COMING TOGETHER AGAIN

The mountain clans have long since scattered
Across the face of the Earth,
Each having been bestowed great gifts -
A glimpse of mountain light,
A taste of mountain springs,
A smell of mountain wildflowers,
The sound of mountain wind,
And the feel of rocky turf beneath bare feet.
I long to be there again
And witness these great things,
To walk among the alpen fields with my kin,
To celebrate with my clan brothers,
And my clan sisters,
To share in the joy
Of knowing that we can always go home in
	high places,
And look down upon the world
And weep,

And laugh,
And come together again.

~

In virtually all of the mountain ranges of the Earth there have been people who have come and gone, many surviving centuries on the gifts that mountains offer – year-round water, deep forests, summer pastures, and ample game. In spite of the harsh weather, the short growing season, and deep winter snows in most mountain ranges, 'mountain people' have survived and even thrived through the years. This poem is dedicated to these people, who have often been a hardier folk, and who have left a legacy of myths, tales, and storied culture.

6

TRACING STEPS

Many have walked here before me.
I step on smooth stones,
Follow the path amidst lichen-encrusted rock,
Strain my eyes in the mist to see the cairns,
Built so long ago,
Built by hand, so very long ago.
Who were these cairn-builders?
These movers of rock,
Defiers of gravity,
Honoring their Scottish stock?
I know not whence they came,
Nor whither their concern,
Only that their rock piles
Have hastened my return,
Some no doubt as history will recount,
Spent their final days stricken upon this
    Mount,

Others have successfully passed this way,
And lived on in the glory of yet another day.
For myself I have followed the truest of paths,
The trail of my own Amidou, upwards at last,
And in but a twinkling, without any idea or
*   inkling,*
That the summit rocks would ever come into
*   view.*
For mine has been the 'nary' path,
'Nary' a cause, and 'nary' a concern,
Only to hold my beliefs in the highest regard,
My heart within the Golden Urn.
And now my fate has been my feet,
Success upon the Mount without defeat,
A cairn-builders tale I can now complete
In honor of those gone before me.

~

Cairns above treeline can mean the difference between life and death in the alpine zone of the Northeast. In a total whiteout where visibility is at best a few meters, even these piles of rock can be too far apart to decipher where the trail lies. In those instances I have relied upon the bareness of smooth walking stones, where the multitudes before me have worn away the moss and lichen covering that otherwise would be encrusting these fell fields. Nowhere was this more evident than on Mount Washington in the White Mountains, where, at age eleven, I scaled my first alpine summit with the help of these cairns. A freak July snowstorm blanketed the Alpine Garden with several inches of snow amidst winds that topped 60 mph. These cairns and the smooth stones between them saved my life as well as those campmates I was with at the time.

7

GRABBING THE PACE

There is a pattern in climbing
And it goes just thus:
One step
And then another,
Grab onto the pace,
And don't get off the bus!

~

This somewhat terse, albeit comical truism about climbing a mountain was born of a mantra that I have used many times in successfully negotiating a long, arduous climb. Although many of the ten or twelve mile approach and return hikes I have done have required such repetitive reminders to hold onto the pace, nowhere was this more evident than when completing the length of the Appalachian Trail in 1973. My brother and I spent five months learning the art of 'grabbing the pace,' which as several thousand others can now attest, is a must if one is to complete this two-thousand mile journey in a single season. Our 131-day trek averaged 16 miles a day, with regular 'get-there' days of over 22 miles.

8

CONDITIONING

Cautious
Careful
Intentional –
Honoring the exercise
Of body, muscle, and breath,
Leaving behind the aged,
Casting off the shroud of death,
For mortal beings that we ever endow
With candor,
And prowess,
And sweat upon the brow,
Shall ever persist as long as we breathe
Beyond the future of the now.
A humbling of power,
A surrender of the mind,
A climber's conditioning loosens the unwind.

~

A bove all else, climbing mountains gets one in good physical shape. Typically, it pushes a climber to the limits of his or her endurance and physical abilities. Yet it also requires a certain presence of mind. The mind also must endure pain and hardship, and remind the body-machine that it is capable of things beyond what it normally accepts as possible. This mind-body interplay during a climb can help alter the beliefs about what is possible, and unwind the self-imposed constraints on physical and mental endurance. I have found this to be particularly important during high stress times when a companion or group is challenged by an unanticipated setback.

9

ELEVEN MILLIMETERS

White-washed stains
On a cliffside high,
A raven's roost
'Gainst the crystal blue sky,
Lichens yielding
To feather and pitch,
A peton's dream
In a quarried stitch,
To know a rope
From braid to bending,
Is to gain a friend
Of life's unending!

This poem honors the rope and all of the limits it has pushed for climbers around the world. My fifty-meter rope has allowed me to gain access to cliffs, ledges, sea caves, and caverns that would have otherwise been impossible to reach. One particular pitch in Baja California was adorned with a raven's nest and a whitewash cliff face that fed bright orange Caloplaca lichens. Whereas the acidic whitewash from the raven's excrement was too harsh to support any lichen or moss growth, just outside the edge of the whitewash was a band of bright orange lichen that relied upon its nutrients in order to survive. I would not have been able to learn of these things without my rope!

10

KICKING STEPS

There is nothing so wonderful
As kicking steps in hard snow –
Each foot
Swinging in perfect unison,
With upward motion,
The energetics -
Streamlined with purpose,
Carving fate deliberately,
One step at a time.
Slowly,
Gaining ground,
Earning the respect
Of the land beneath,
Conquering
Not the summit,
But the gravity of the soul.
The mountain yields itself easily under such
    acts.

~

There is a certain meditation when kicking steps in hard snow. For anyone who has done this, and a single high-elevation mountain almost always requires it, the boredom and monotony of it will boggle if not break the mind. For those of us who have climbed in snow and ice under all kinds of conditions, those perfectly pitched slopes with perfect snow are ones we all seek and remember well. One of those for me was the north face of Popocateptl in central Mexico. In what was one of the most perfect mountain cones I have ever ascended, the four-thousand foot slope below the crater was one of the longest yet easiest ascents I have had on account of such perfect conditions. Rarely have I or most climbers I know been so blessed!

11

SNOW ON HIGH

Like watery down
It brushes my wind-blown face,
Slowly at first,
Then with a quickening pace,
Heart racing,
A long ways yet to go,
Ice fields now slick
The kick steps are slow.
The Mountain rejoices
In spite of my pacing,
For its marriage to cloud
Is well worth embracing.
I cut into the side slope
And fashion a cave,
Slip into my down scape
And relinquish the day.
Bring what weather and wind,
That make the ridges glow,

With rime ice and hoar frost
And ever present snow.

~

This poem was inspired by a winter ascent of Mount Rainier. My traveling mates were prepared for the worst and the worst was what the mountain offered up that day with a full-blown winter storm coming in by the time we were about two hours up from Paradise Lodge. Well-prepared, we dug in our snow cave and nestled into what would be a long night, with a rotating duty set up to carve out an air hole to make sure we didn't suffocate before dawn.

PART II
THE ASCENT

THE ASCENT

12

BLOCKING SPACE

As if
Every,
Moment,
Mattered.
This how I'd like to live my life.
Remembering sometimes,
In the face of incredible danger –
Like that impossibly long,
Lightening fast slide down a glacier,
Or that point of ultimate surrender
On the cliff face of Mount Ranger,
Or finding the wreckage of that plane
And imagining the death of a stranger –
These are the moments that define us,
That give us the luxury of measuring space,
Of blocking out time,
Burning memories we can never erase,
No matter how sublime.

What makes it thus,
Our path,
Our destiny,
To Live or to Die,
A life well worth the pace of passing by?
Tis the ability to know
Just how it all works,
To witness the peaks
And where love's labor lurks,
To partition the thread
Of Fate and its quirks,
And rejoice in the capture
Of a moment or two,
And face into the wind
To steer hard the rudder through.

～

This poem honors every moment in the mountains when the face of death has impressed upon me a memory that lasts a lifetime. In the 1970's I found the wreck of a Cessna aircraft high in the Olympics, miles from anywhere, yet unquestionably fatal for both passengers. Later that decade on Mount Ranger I faced a downclimb that was impossible below a sharp overhang with no rope to stop a two hundred foot fall. My third and final mountaineering brush with death took place on the north face of Mount Rainier where, after foolishly assuming an unseen snowfield would submit to my ice axe in a nice long glissade, I encountered sheer ice that sent me careening downslope at speeds in excess of twenty miles an hour regardless of the arrest position I held. Layers of skin peeled off an arm or leg every time I encountered a high spot. I finally stopped ten feet from the rocks when deeper snows allowed me to resist the fall. These moments - certainly not confined to mountaineering but perhaps more common there – are those that seem to 'block time,' lock in memory, and remind us of our own mortality.

13

BIRTH OF A STREAM

Tumbling down
Like feather breath
The mist
Envelops the crown,
Dew-laden tears
Drop deeply now,
Shedding sorrow
Mournfully,
Changing
The color of a painted rock
As it slowly turns to soil.
The passage of
Everlasting rain
Reflects
The ringlets of this sweet refrain,
As wayward as the droplets may seem,
The path of water,
In the mountains,

Always
Gives birth
To the stream.

~

Clouds tell of the inevitable birthplace of every rivulet, brook, stream, and great river on Earth. Born of the high places on this 'water planet,' flowing water always originates from the aggregation of precipitation, whether it be the base of some unknown glacier, the surging spring at the face of some crack in a rock, or the simple path of one scoured gully joining another. Even desert mountains have shed water in this way, slowly perhaps, but always exhibiting the downcut pattern of water-driven erosion. When climbing, water and the availability of it can determine everything–from one's ability to traverse a certain area, to the types of rotten or slippery rock one will encounter on a cliff face, to whether or not a mountain is even attainable if water must be carried the entire way.

14

BENDING LIGHT

It came in on a new wind,
That cloak of icy fog,
Settling like a blanket over a frigid, barren
    landscape.
Misty rain
Crystallizing new skin
On bark, rock, and frame,
At first very thin,
Layer after layer, building
Then sagging, everything.
And then it cleared.
The dawning brought into sharp focus
Silvery, shimmering prisms,
A sparkling fire,
Alighting the stark and somber wood
    unmatched
By anything in winter's attire.
I walk through a crystalline palace

Of Nature's design,
Oblivious of cold, frozen in time.

And then it begins, slowly at first,
With quickening pace,
The sun has burst through the clouds, now
   warming
The heart of the glaze,
Bringing heat to the face.
A slight, small crackle or two,
The wind responds in kind,
And whips the heat through,
What was once quite still,
A blazing rhinestone hush,
Is now a clattering fury,
A gathering crush.
Pelted by ice drops and icicle rain,
The forest shakes off
Its pendulous mane.
Relieved of its burden,
A broken branch refrain,
An Ice Storm has plundered New England
Once more and again.

~

lthough not necessarily confined to mountains, ice storms can absolutely change the face of a forest and awaken us to a different kind of disaster. Most common in narrow bands of elevation on the sides of a mountain or hill, a slight differential in temperature can lock in place freezing clouds upon the surface of the Earth. Once complete, although beautiful to behold and often sparkling in the clearing sun, the damage wrought by such a storm can absolutely shudder the power to a community. This poem reflects upon one of the two major ice storms to hit New England in the last twenty years, one in 1998 that took down major international powerlines between Quebec and New England, and one in 2008 that caused power outages that lasted up to a month or more.

15

MOUNTAIN WIND TRAINS

Here they come again
Descending from on high,
Cascading down
Sweeping the treetops
A relentless sound is nigh,
Like so many trains rushing
This way and that
A perilous path gushing
Branches broken and cracked,
All ice flying
Bullets from the sky
Pelting snow drifts
With an icicle eye,
Reddening skin
Like so many lashes
Snow dust everywhere
Frozen firebox ashes,
I long for a sleep

Oh give me my fur
I'll head for the deep
My den to inter,
I'll pray for my kin
Look out at the stars
Dancing again
The story from afar,
A mountain's tale can never be told
Without wind trains and whistles, and
unrelenting cold.

~

I was inspired to write this by winter winds in the mountains that come to visit my home every December and stay on as unwanted guests until April every year. Living at the base of the "front range" of the White Mountains as I do, I mark the day when the arctic blast has settled on high to the north, and then proceeds to drop precipitously down the three and a half thousand feet to my back yard. I listen as these 'wind trains' pass through and every time recall the hours spent hunkered down on some alpine ridge where such winds have kept me tent-bound. After many hours and even days on end for some mountaineers, one cannot help but think of the advantage of bears in their winter dens. Yet for those that choose to brave the elements of winter on a mountainside, these are not uncommon occurrences. They remind us of how we as humans are poorly adapted to the vagaries of mountain weather.

16

POPOCATEPETL

The pale blue moonlight bore the stillness
Like a wedding gown,
Proud, ethereally beautiful, anticipatory.
None of us knew it would happen.
A distant rumble from deep below,
Like the sound of the metro four stories down,
Descended from the crater above,
A slight trembling at first,
Then louder,
Trees shivering,
All animals now running away this way and
        that,
Owls taking flight from the pines in the night,
A gentle wind ushering the earth quake in.
Then a moment of silence,
As if the introductions were made,
The forest's applause fell silent,
All was still in the dappled shade.

Then the wave came.
The deep rumbling resumed,
Faster now,
Louder, and louder,
Like a freight train bearing down hard,
It threw us into the air like rag dolls,
Three, maybe four feet above
A crest of earth that broke downhill,
A wave of earth traveling as fast as a wave in
    the sea,
But this one pounding down towards the
    unsuspecting valley,
Trees and limbs flying,
Bare earth cracked wide open,
Boulders settling into new chasms,
The maw of the mountainside
Shredded,
Its legions of trees newly embedded,
Soon settling down back again,
Reconstructed, somewhat askew, yet quiet,
As if nothing ever happened.
We watched as the lights went out in the valley
    below,
Watched as the wave snuffed out the
    twinkling,
Snuffed out lives,
Watched as the valley grew dark,
Silent,
Ominous,
Nothing moving here or there now,
All quiet, yet morbidly disastrous.

It took a while before car lights, yellow then
    red and blue,
Began racing across the valley again,
Lots of distant sirens, flashing lights, horns,
As the toll of ten thousand lives began to be
    counted.
We lingered awake long into the night,
Unable to sleep,
Unable to move,
Expecting, perhaps,
Another wave, a deepening rent in the Earth
That would swallow us whole.
None ever came.
Instead, we considered our options as we
    attempted sleep in the twilight.
Dawn broke and the sun shone bright on us
    and our comrades,
A dozen or so witnesses to this unfathomable
    event,
Sitting up on the high ridge of this once again
    active volcano,
Knowing full well we were lucky to be alive.
We told stories,
Ate sparingly,
Conferred with the ranger on patrol,
Who was begging into his walkie-talkie:
    'Ayudarme, ayudarme!'
To help him check on his family in the village
    below,
We watched him drive away only to be stopped
By the fractured road in splinters far below,

*Leaving his truck and running downhill at full
speed,
Miles from nowhere, from his family, from the
clouds of dust
That were everywhere below.
Yes, we gave thanks,
Shared in the blessings of being up here,
At the start of it all,
Surrounded by a wilderness without walls,
With ample food, water, and stories to recall,
To bathe in the camaraderie of the other lucky
souls
Who had made the journey as well,
And came out whole!*

~

In December 1972 a magnitude 6.5 earthquake struck Central America with one of its epicenters on the west side of Popocatepetl in central Mexico. I had just finished soloing up this 17,887-foot high peak, the second highest in the country. My partner and I rested on the *altiplano* between Popo and Iztacihuatl, the slightly smaller volcano to the north when the earthquake struck. Although both of us had experienced earth tremors and quakes before, neither of us had been at the epicenter, let alone on the side of a volcano where the tremor had caused a wave of solid earth to descend the mountainside. While in our sleeping bags comfortably asleep, we were awoken by the earth trembling beneath us and watched as it increased in pressure and intensity, and then fell silent. Thinking all was safe we sat up and then watched seconds later a four-foot high wave sweep down past us and throw us in the air. We stared in amazement as it rolled downhill like a small tsunami causing chaos and disruption everywhere. Fewer than five minutes later it struck the valley with a devastating blow to all structures. Thousands of lives were lost in a matter of minutes. Sharing our shock and grief with other climbers in the morning the next day, we all felt lucky to be alive.

17

RETRIBUTION ARÊTE

There must be a path
How silly of me
To think that a knife edge
Would yield us so easily.
From afar the ridge look flat and long,
Now approaching its base
I see I was wrong,
For spires and chimneys are lined up in rows,
Like some absurd cluster of gargoyle toes,
The traverse would now take all of our time
That was supposed to be dedicated to the
        summit cone climb,
A tyrolean perhaps would lessen the blow
To our calculated plans made so far below,
Let's hope the rope holds onto the solid wall
And ferries us safely beyond the great fall!

~

This poem reflects on one of many times a mountain climbing plan went badly awry. Back before GPS and aerial imagery and GoogleEarth 3D was available, I set out with friend to ascend the west face of Mount Constance in the Olympic Mountains of western Washington. I had climbed this second-highest peak before, but never from this direction. Our planned route took us across a relatively short east-west arête that separated the west face from our bivouac camp. Once at its start we realized quickly that it was not as flat or wide as expected. With my inexperienced climbing friend on board, I knew I would have to simplify the crossing for him, and so set up a Tyrolean traverse in order to more easily skirt the knife edge 'sawteeth.' Although successful, this ended up costing us valuable time that forced a number of unexpected events to ensure (see next two poems).

18

A SPIDER'S TALE

Did it ever occur to me that the cliff was so tall
*   and so exposed?*
The talus bore the truth of the unstable rock
*   above,*
All broken and sharp from gravity's little shove,
Flying bits of stony shrapnel pummeled the
*   steepening slope,*
Yet I ascended the crumbling scree in spite of
*   little hope.*

Once at the cliff face
I heaved a sigh of relief,
Until I looked up,
And realized the respite was all too brief,
For there laid in front of me
Was an unending series of cracks
And once I was committed
There was no turning back,

So I chose what appeared then
To be the longest running track,
Of vertical granite columns,
Stack after stack.
For a while it was easy in the faded setting sun,
To opposition climb the vertical chimney run,
But as soon as I saw the summit's shoulder up
    ahead,
The way was overhung by an enormous jutting
    head,
At this point the promise of passage sunk into
    the faceless void,
The sun had cast its final shadow and the light
    I once enjoyed.
With knees now trembling hard
And fingers in numbing pain
I cast a glance towards the Earth
Where loose rock fell again,
I knew this was it,
The final moment where time and space were
    true,
When there by my side,
With an unhurried stride,
A spider came into view.
I imagined its place,
Amidst the world of horizontal and vertical
    planes,
And how the rock was covered with holds
Where eight legs could make their gains.
Taking a breath I knelt deep into the rock
And effected a crawling pose,
Closing my eyes I tried to take stock

Of the minutia beneath my toes,
Three points secure, I cast out my lure
For a fourth upon which to land,
Shifting my web, with an arachnid gait,
I slowed time beneath the sand.
Slowly I crept from crevice to crack
And gained the overhanging ledge
Never looking back,
Until I could put my fully booted foot
In a chimney beneath the shoulder's edge.
The summit was alit in an eerie orange glow
From light in the western sky,
Though I could not tarry long
I thanked spider and its kin
For teaching me how not to die.

~

C ontinuing down from the arête I left my climbing companion on the side of a small glacier with adequate water and gear to survive the night if need be, and headed to the west face. This poem tells of my encounter with this route, which was advertised as a doable 5.4, yet turned out to contain a couple of 5.8 maneuvers high up on the upper part of the face. Since the Tyrolean had delayed the onset of the cliff climb, the sun was setting when I reached the 'rate determining step' of this ascent. Hours of hiking and rock work had weakened my knees and it was apparent I had made the unwise decision to solo up an unexplored route in the dwindling light. The visual from below did not reveal the overhang until I was upon it. Perhaps I had lost the published route or perhaps it was inaccurate, it didn't matter. I had reached a point when a downclimb was far more dangerous (read: invisible) than continuing on, when a spider came across my view. If I only had eight legs, I thought. Nonetheless, the reminder about the right approach provided me with the grace to carry on, surmount the overhang, and attain the summit. My brief celebration was punctuated by the obvious dilemma of it growing quickly dark and me being miles away from my climbing partner! (see next poem)

19

FLIGHT OF FANCY

Swaying back and forth
In a tree-top moon,
The feel of the rock
Could not come too soon,
Closer and closer
I set the bough,
To kiss the cliff
With heathered brow,
A strategic leap
Was my midnight plan,
To reach the ledge
And start climbing again,
Though shear down below
Was this mountain's side,
At canopy height
It shoulders were wide,
With one last crouch
I sprang from the fir,

As dark green met gray
My flight was a blur,
Til vibram met stone
Where resistance was nigh,
And gravity lost ground
To the never-ending sky,
Although the feat worked
And the obstacle was overcome,
I left part of my soul there
To wait for the noonday sun.

∽

The sun had long set before I had completed a desperate run down the main trail up Mount Constance. I reached the elevation where I needed to break off and return north to the valley below the west face, and reascend the ridge behind which my companion had agreed to meet me. The subalpine valley was largely clear of vegetation, but when I approached the north end I found a solid line of trees below a sheer cliff 60 - 100 feet high. It was nearly dark now, so visibility was poor and I was beginning to cramp up from the 14 hours of exertion and little food. I saw no way up the cliff and no way around it. Instead, I chose to find the lowest point and climb a subalpine fir tree at its base and ascend to the top and swing over to the upper part of the ledge. This poem is about the success of that maneuver. This put me on top of the ledge, which was now bathed in a growing moonlight that lit my way across the ridge back to the rendezvous point.

Although at this point I thought all was good, I did not realize that my climbing companion had made an unwise decision to move from the rendezvous point and start heading back in the direction of the bivouac camp. He not only headed in the wrong direction, but managed to fall into a bergschrund, knock himself out, and almost die of hypothermia in the process. After I completed a two hour search, he came around enough to let out a low moan that allowed me to find him. I was able to get a fire going and warm him up enough to get him back moving again in spite of a broken arm and cracked rib. Somehow we both managed to survive this climb that should have killed us both.

20

OF DISTANT SHORES

I climb inside a capsule of time
A windowless world now awaits me,
My transport is fast through this terran
*   looking glass*
Til I sit on the shores of a vast sea.
Sediments surround, the volcanoes have all
*   drowned*
Turbidity currents lie around me,
I wander among the iron-clad lungs
Of creatures that crawl and don't see.
What masterful art these colors will impart
Upon a canvas of seabed stratigraphy,
The very flakes that I find, now back in present
*   time,*
Carry the essence of geological history.
Bone fiber black, a biotite fleck,
Of a ferro-magnesial mystery,
Can now be divined among lava laden lines

That ripple across the porphyry.
I stand only to gain from this rock detective
     game,
For minerals are what's deep inside me,
To know where I've been and what I will
     become
Yields comfort amidst the asynchrony.
Tis true,
The mountains beget what we must never
     forget,
That our ingredients of biological necessity,
Came from scattered dust and the stars we
     entrust
With the mixing of metasedimentary mystery.

~

Nowhere on the Earth has the complexity of the bedrock been so evident to me as in the Olympic Mountains of western Washington. The twists and folds are as convoluted as any bed of metamorphosed schist that I have seen. These old seabed sediments carry the tale of continents crashing and seas uplifting into lofty mountains several thousands of feet high, and yet are fresh enough to reveal their making in the minerals that have been crushed, reformed, and extruded in layer after layer. This poem highlights the interplay between these events, and reminds the reader about the source of minerals within our bodies that both give us life and connect us to the stars from which we came.

21

WONDROUS ART

I often wonder in my wandering,
How the canvas beneath my feet will look
    today?
What alchemy will transform
The reds, greens, blues, and browns
Into
Firs,
Carpets of moss,
Glacial ice,
And snow algae,
All perfectly composed,
Brushed in with perfection,
Dappled with light,
Smoothed by a mountain mist,
That strokes in and out
Across the treetops,
Wreathing bits of magic as it goes.

~

This poem honors the artistry of creation amidst all of the elements of Earth. Mountain climbing often reveals such artistry and allows us to think about and appreciate the diversity of life that surrounds. At the very least, 'marking time' by observing the aesthetic interplay between the 'cloak of life' and the mountain's ethers is worthy of exploration.

22

DIXVILLE PEAK

Dixville Peak: A Mountain by Any Other Name

A spruce-fir thicket
So dense,
I could look back and see where I'd been
A half-hour ago.
Pathways were everywhere, though
Made by rabbits, martens, squirrels -
They were impossibly small.
In my mind I was still a Lilliputian,
Yet my scarred and bleeding limbs told me
I was still a giant.

The climb had been easy.
Massive yellow birch,
Welcoming limbs that reached the ground,
Hobbit holes everywhere,
Faery condominiums in every upturned root.

In my mind I was a Lilliputian,
Yet my clumsy, flower-stomping feet told me
I was still a giant.

On the ridge we came upon a trail,
And I could breathe again.
Foot travel eased,
And the forest flew by.
The ground became soft, moist.
Mushrooms were everywhere,
All colors of the rainbow appeared,
As if Alice was waiting there,
In my mind I was a Lilliputian,
Yet after bending low to inspect the
        spotted one
I was still a giant.

And then there was nothing
But space and scarred ground,
Brown scorched earth all around,
Cut trees tossed this way and that,
The marr of bulldozer blades' fat,
All life extinguished,
All sounds silenced,
Except that of a big whirring blade,
Pushing power out of the wind,
One of a string in along parade,
Two hundred feet tall,
I was indeed a Lilliputian now
Living a life so very small!

~

For many long years the remoteness of mountains have withstood the travails of civilization. In the Northeast, this has begun to change. Outside of the well-known icons of Mount Washington, Mount Monadnock, Cadillac Mountain and the like – mountains in general have been the destination of foot travelers and the home of a myriad of animals, plants, and fungi that live there undisturbed year-round. Climbing Dixville Peak in the north country of New Hampshire has reminded me that the once secure remoteness of a distant peak can now be overcome by machinery. In a land where such a viewless summit has largely been the home of small creatures that can easily pass, bulldozers, excavators, and cranes have made it possible for such peaks to be the home of a new resident, one that captures wind to drive the power to support an encroaching civilization. Four major wind arrays now exist in the state, and each of these are less than twenty years old. At least four more are on the planning books, one of which is proposed for floating ocean mounts. In this poem I had to wonder while crawling through a forest suitable for an animal no bigger than a snowshoe hare, what kind of future have we imparted on the mountains of the world with our increasingly sophisticated technology?

PART III
THE TRAVERSE

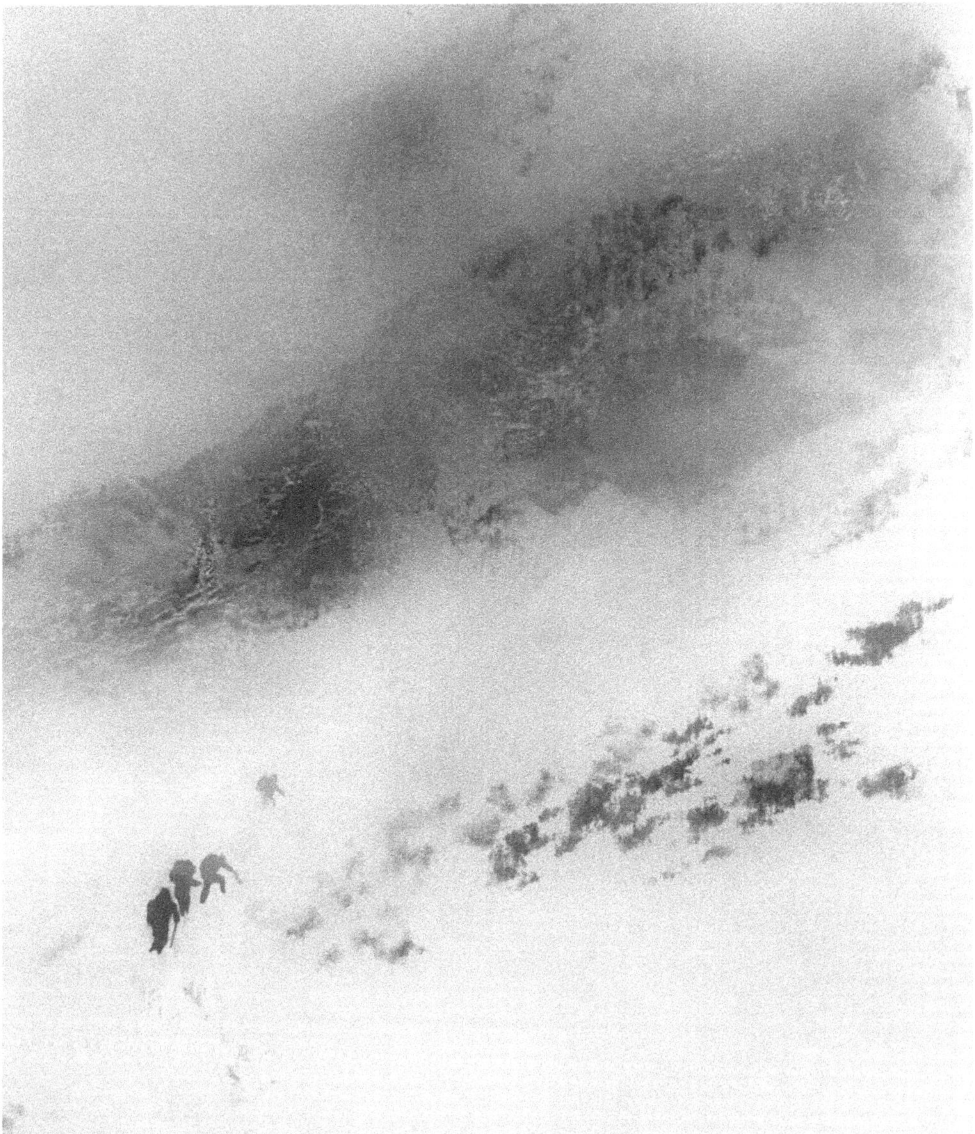

THE TRAVERSE

23

A SPIRIT ENGAGED

I come then
To the Mountain
Not to quest or
To train or
To summit or any of these things –
I come to the mountain
To engage the spirit of the place,
To learn from its wisdom,
To sing its song,
To dance its dance,
To walk in the footsteps
Of our ancestors who did these things,
To drink from crystal clear springs,
To breathe fresh air,
And to walk among the flowers there.

∾

A mountain's traverse can be a time to relax for a moment, having attained a certain altitude and achieved through skill and endurance the right to look back at the successes that got you there and look ahead at the challenges you yet face. Consequently, the traverse often allows the climber the brief luxury of reflecting on the spiritual journey of climbing a mountain. While uncertainty still lies ahead – including the 'rate determining step, a certain degree of reward confirms the assuredness of being in the right place at the right time. For those not interested in attaining the summit, this is often the point at which the climber has attained his or her destination and needs to travel no more.

24

A MOUNTAIN AT-ONE-MENT

From lofty crags
Clear vision,
Dancing clouds,
Life in revision,
To make myself even better still
I drink from the pool of an icy rill,
Plunge in a tarn,
Chew glacier lily leaves,
Whistle back at marmots,
Or pikas if you please,
The way of the climber is not about the top,
Instead it's about knowing exactly where to
    stop,
Gathering dew,
Burrowing down,
Delphinium blue,
Alders all around,
I am filled with a joy a passerby cannot know,

*I am one with the mountain with miles yet
to go.*

$\sim$

I was inspired to write this after a recent traverse of Heney Ridge in central Alaska where miles upon miles of unbroken and untrammeled terrain lay in front of me. At the end of the trail the choices were limitless. With snow-clad peaks in every direction, the temptation was to pick one and summit. Instead, I spent hours investigating the world above treeline, grazing on huckleberries, glacier lilies and springwater, nestling into the warm earth facing an all too brief sun shower, and bathing in an icy tarn. Becoming a part of this world in every way possible was my goal for the day, to learn of its mysteries, to feel its power, and to return renewed as if I had just had a good visit with an old friend.

25

FELSENMEER

Cast upon the shores of cloud and stone,
I wander with Oetzi in the mist alone,
The winds of fate have brought us both here,
To live and die upon the felsenmeer.
Like the tide that draws upon the sea,
His death has kindled the alpine in me,
What was it like to die in that glacial grip?
Did he know his flight was a one-way trip?
From a lowland fog and its heavier air,
And the threat of mankind that has shunned
us there,
A life above treeline is where we can get free,
And set up our camp in the mountain's lee,
Then follow the path of deep sublimity,
Rest upon moss and gathering dream,
And seek the righteous life or so it would
seem.

*Still the felsenmeer beckons me back into the
      fold,
Of a deepening history, a story untold,
Of seeker, and wind, and incarcerating cold.
Deep in the heart of the mountain they say,
Walks a nameless soul who has lost his way,
Who was shot by an arrow and staggered away,
Only to die without fire or ceremony,
But through me has come yet to live another
      day.*

~

This poem recalled my visit to Oetzi, the five
thousand year-old man found in an alpine glacier,
who lived among a clan of mountain people in what
is now the Italian Alps. Humans, having gained agriculture
through the domestication of grain and livestock at that time,
could now live in a harsh and forbidding environment such as
the Alps. Whether for summer pasturage, hunting game, or
gathering herbs, these mountain people were the forbearers of
a culture of 'mountain folk' that occupied high places for
thousands of years. While ascending a 3,000 meter peak near
where Oetzi was found, I could only imagine what life was like
then, and how razor sharp the skills of survival were for these
people.

26

ON THE BRINK

The maw of the two thousand foot precipice
Stretches far down below me,
I waver a little in place,
Tempting fate,
Feeling gravity,
Imagining the rush of wind,
The impact at over two hundred miles an hour
        far below.
One moment upright, living,
The next, scattered, in pieces, dead.
What draws men to test such fear?
Why do mountains put us,
Our spirits on the line,
On the brink of a new awakening?

~

U ltimately we must all die. This fact is burned into our DNA as vividly as the breath of life itself. Mountain climbing often brings us to this point of embracing our own mortality. Many climbers do not return home. Short of military service, there are few sectors of society where such a realization is more palpably present. I have often wondered, does staring death in the face make us feel more alive? Why do people choose to engage in such a risk? While it is most assuredly different for every individual that undertakes such a challenge, there is no doubt a common thread of understanding that to be alive in the face of death is a graceful gift worth living for.

THE HIGHLAND THAT I LOVE

On the highland I find a peculiar quest
To live as a species completely undressed,
To touch ancient bones of rock and root,
To dress up my body in a cool mossy suit,
To swim with the fish in a shadowed hole,
To crawl in the mud like some mischievous
    mole,
To eat of the fruits of fungus and vine,
And drink from the stills of geologic time.
For mine is the path in honor of the Earth,
For which I have no tears, no laughter or
    mirth,
For the way of the seeker is deliberate and true,
Intentional, exact, like fresh morning dew.
On a mountain the quest is at its absolute best,
Where leadership and humility are part of the
    test,

*Where the trust that we seek can find its way
    home,
To the heart of another on the mountain
    alone,
That which binds the soul can ne'er be
    undone,
As with life or death, or the brilliance of
    the sun.*

~

Being in the mountains can inspire us, even require us to be more fully ourselves. We are often so far outside of ourselves that we have forgotten exactly how to be. Climbing can put us in touch with our elemental nature in a way that brings us home to the truth of being alive, aware, intact, and at peace with who we are. I have found a greater sense of being alive as well as a greater sense of camaraderie in the mountains. Honoring the highlands that have brought this about was the singular purpose of this poem.

MOUNTAIN COMFORT

Rest your soul upon my lap,
And let your worries go,
Find peace inside a gentle nap,
For I am with you now,
A chalice of comfort I offer to thee
To ease that which is sore,
Drink deep of my crystalline reverie,
And let your mind explore.
Nestle into my mossy down,
Breathe in my earthen aires,
Quiet your mind of raucous sounds,
And release all of your cares.
For my heart is your heart,
Within my chest interred,
My soul is now your soul,
Our union ne'er deterred.

∾

There are times when the comfort of being high up on the mountain can seem impossibly right. These are the rare moments when a world that is normally harsh, auspicious, and tragic lets down its guard and accepts a climber into its fold. Warmth, food, and shelter is secure, and a peaceful respite on the 'Mount' can be had. While altogether brief, these moments can embody a connection that is typically missing from traveling across a foreign land.

29

THE NAMELESS MOUNTAIN

There is nothing quite like it.
I have been there. I know I have –
Or so it must verily seem,
Of all of God's creatures on Earth and beyond
A mountain is more like a dream,
Palpable, yet distant, with characters
    proclaiming
Lines from a long ago scene,
The mountain imagines itself a seeker
Where none has ever been,
The highlands draw the spirit forth
Like a moth unto a flame,
The climber knows the risks he takes
And the rules of gravity's game,
For 'ere the summit finds the trekker alone
Whose legs have all gone lame,
Awareness seeps into the mind of the believer –
Life will never be the same.

Arise my friends and greet the dawn
From a mountaintop retreat,
And rest your eyes upon the burgeoning skies,
Gold clouds beneath your feet,
Let mind and body drift away
On graceful wings of sleep,
And feel the mountain's molten core
Many miles beneath your seat,
For nothing stands any higher now,
No longer your heart to beat,
A welcome land awaits you here,
You've found just what you seek.

~

This poem moves the imagination from the mountain dream into a forever world. It invites the reader to visualize traversing a high away place, and to awaken into a golden dawn beyond physical reality. For those who have died and come back, and for those who are able to experience life beyond the dream, the mountain offers up a perfect metaphor for transitioning into the spirit realm. I have found that practicing such 'mountain meditation' helps in accepting my own mortality as well as the mortality of others who have already passed beyond this life.

30

LOOK TO THE DAWN

*The end of each day comes quickly on the
    mountaintop.*
*Where the air is thin, and the stars are much
    brighter,*
*Nightfall is hastened more quickly here than
    anywhere else.*
*One minute the rosy hues of twilight are cast
    upon the snowfields,*
*The next they are a deep and somber blue-
    purple,*
As if the curtain has fallen on a majestic stage,
*And the lingering spotlights on the highest
    peaks have proceeded to turn their page.*
I mourn the loss of such light,
As it is such a mystical, magical sight,
When the painted canvas grows dim,
And the last thrush has gone within,
I fall into a deep and restful sleep,

Awaiting, like on Christmas Eve,
The bugling of dawn's light on snowy peaks!

~

This passage honors all of the countless times a summit attempt was foiled and then, miraculously, like a lucky hand at cards, everything lines up perfectly for the final summit climb. The air of anticipation becomes palpable even as it softens the blow of witnessing a quickening nightfall. For the promise of another day, and one perhaps filled with glory and success, overcomes the climber who is now feeling hopeful for a fruitful tomorrow.

THE SUMMIT CONE

THE SUMMIT CONE

The summit cone's rim,
Jagged teeth protruding,
Snowfields blinding light,
The path fairly easy now.
Rocks have fallen,
Taken out a comrade or two,
Our rope has been the lucky one,
To carry four climbers through.
The rest returned as we marched in step,
Like a tethered octo-ped,
It was all about the altitude now,
Less oxygen in our heads.
The sun had softened a well-worn path
Round rim and fumarole,
The wind had slackened across the flats,
And released the sulphuric hole.
Crest after crest fell away before me
As we learned the mountain's tune,

From an icy chill in the depths of a crevasse
To a T-shirt stroll in June.
Rainier has taken its share of lives,
From the seasoned to the unprepared,
This time the Whittaker-Gombu belays
Ensured how well we fared.
A snow bridge skip
That melted fast,
Meant one less road for the return,
The dance upon the bergschrund's lip,
Showed Nawang's lack of concern.
The green felt cap was ever ahead
Upon the fisted brow,
Until the top was well within reach,
And a voice said, "It's time to turn back now!"
Querulous looks befit the party
Until our gaze looked west,
For thereupon a midsummer's calm
A gathering storm changed our quest.
The Chinook relinquished its temperate hold
On the summit and its melted cone,
When a northerly gale stepped up its pace
To chill us to the bone.
The rain slanted in and iced the crest
Returning crampons to our feet,
The sodden ropes were slicker now
And boot belays no easy feat.
Our hardy crew knew just what to do,
In step we were by then,
With Nawang's laugh and smiling face
And mountaineering zen.
The descent to Muir went quickly by

In spite of soaking winds,
The stony hut was full of cheer
Regaled by survivor's grins.
The storm abated and we returned in kind
On freshly fallen snow,
Glissading down to Paradise
Was worth the summit show!

~

This poem was inspired by my first ascent of Mount Rainier in western Washington state. At age seventeen it was my first real ascent of any large peak, and although only fourteen thousand feet high, it felt like Everest to me. What was equally as noteworthy as the 'turn-back' weather that arrived while we sat halfway around the summit cone, was the fact that the only two rope teams that made it up before the storm that day was led by two Everest summiteers, Jim Whittaker and Nawang Gombu. Both were part of the successful Everest climb in 1963, where Willi Unsoeld, Barry Bishop, and Tom Hornbein completed a first ascent of the West Ridge, and Jim and Nawang had already made the top using the South Col route. Gombu was the only person at that time to have summited Everest twice, and here he was leading our four-person rope with ski poles! It appeared to be an easy walk-up for him!

32

A MOUNTAINS' PENANCE

Time is too quick
For mortals to care
'Bout the ancient life
Of mountains so fair,
We've all traversed them
At least in mind's eye,
And drawn from their breath
A star-studded sky,
Oh lofty range of pinnacled peaks,
You know all too well of that which I speak,
Though the curse of continents has lifted you
    high,
You're left to suffer the fate
Of never reaching the sky.
For a mountain's tale can never be told,
For those without memory,
Will never grow old.

~

This poem belies the fact that we as humans cannot really grapple with the concept of 'mountain time.' Our short span of living is less than one-thousandth of one percent of the time it takes to form most mountains, let alone erode them away. This is not unlike trying to reach the stars by climbing a mountain. Such a perspective cannot help but to humble us as a species as we tell our story to the world, sometimes while trying to make our species out to be "god's gift."

33

GOOD PROSPECTS

How many Prospect Mountains are there?
Does the view offer a prospect?
Or does the mountain itself offer good
    prospecting?
Or do the 'pros' expect/suspect/inspect the
    mountain itself?
I'm not sure if I have ever done any of these
    when negotiating a mountain.
For the Mountain lies not for itself,
Nor for any man –
It is but a symbol for all that we strive for,
All that is,
And all that can be.
It is a symbol of the self and the selfless,
That which we seek to be yet cannot be,
A goal, an objective, a plan, and a target,
Yet once reached, none of these things at all.
In truth, the mountain rests its soulful head

Upon the roots of non-existence.

~

his reflection is my humble attempt to understand the 'zen' of a mountain and our myriad reasons for climbing them. It was borne of a hike up a "Prospect Mountain" near where I live, wherein I mused about the origins of the word, 'prospect.' For me, the secret to a good prospect on the mountain is embedded in an ability to become thoroughly unattached to one self.

34

METAL OF HONOR

Cast from deep within the Earth
With heat reforged
A purposeful delivery
From one galaxy to the next,
A symbol of courage and hope,
Of everlasting power,
Honor bestows upon itself,
Honor.
There was a time of Man, however,
When leaving one's mark
Was looked down upon,
When footprints were too heavy,
And spirit walked freely between
The mortal realms,
When honor begat
True Honor.
Those days are long gone, however,
These days are so different now.

Men battle men for honor,
Men use power for honor,
Men rule over women for honor,
And men seek the stars for honor.
Yet what was once lost needs to be refound,
Neither in the sky nor in the ground.
That which is palpable must be made
    untouchable,
That which is gold must be turned back to
    lead,
That which now seems right in the world
Must be transformed yet again
Into true Honor,
The Honor of knowing,
The Honor of being wise,
The Honor of being one with All that is.

~

This narrative analyzes the interplay between apparent 'honor' versus 'true honor.' Apparent honor has begotten things such as metals that have been mined out of the Earth to elevate men above the Earth itself. The mark of one's prowess, not unlike climbing to the summit of a mountain itself, is but a falsehood if the end alone justifies the means. 'True' honor is felt and not worn, it is a process and not a goal, a way of being and not an achievement in and of itself. The mark of someone with true honor is not observable in the records of the summits s/he has bagged or the obstacles s/he has overcome; rather, it is observable in the legacy of inspiration s/he has left behind.

35

SEEDS OF FATE

High above
The wispy clouds
Dancing on rocks
Like a pipit on the fells,
I watch the gentle down fly past,
An aspen's dream of a winter that will not last,
Remarkable
The fate
Of seeds from down below,
Testing,
Investing,
In a gait that redefines 'slow,'
For one day, perhaps
In a vastly misshapen world
The daisy
And the dandelion
Will inherit the alpen furl.

~

I was inspired to write this while sauntering through budding alpine wildflowers in the Wind River Range in Wyoming several years ago. A lone aspen seed came floating by at twelve thousand feet, and I wondered about its fate. In fact, it made me think of all of the windborne seeds that make their way up from the lowlands only to land in what would otherwise seem like an inhospitable environment. After hand-picking dandelions from the top of Mount Washington this past year, I have been reminded of the fact that our alpine "proving grounds" may be shifting as the global climate warms and weather patterns result in a softening of harsh alpine conditions.

36

LONG FORGOTTEN KIN

When trees summoned the breeze
And flowers charmed the bees,
When stones were fashioned into bones
And water sang lullabies to the sky,
I was there,
I was there.
I was there when mountains first cast off soil,
And leaves decayed into deep beds of oil,
When life forms were fueled by rays of the sun,
And consciousness had only just begun.
I was there,
I was there.
I was there when scales changed into skin,
And Raven flew to the Sun and back again,
When the four-leggeds became the two-leggeds
And monkeys became men,
When the stars in my lovers eyes begat
A billion people again and again.

I was there,
I was there.
I am here now at the verge of worldly collapse,
People wander in the darkness, seeking light,
Or forgiveness perhaps.
We have forgotten who we are and from
      whence we once came,
And what lies within our spirit beyond the
      name.
For we have strayed from the One so far since
      it has begun,
That all we see is black and white in the
      noonday sun,
Yet the pink-fingered rays of dawn can bring
      back color to the eye,
And knowledge of the fact that we shall
      never die,
They shall transform the life force within our
      hearts,
And begin life anew with a brand new start,
I was there then,
And I am here now,
And forever shall I honor Earth's kinship vow.

∼

This poem honors all of the ages of life on Earth, from its very first rudimentary beginnings to the present day where one species, *Homo sapiens*, is threatening the very existence of all life on Earth. If I have learned anything from climbing mountains and gaining a distant but necessary perspective on humankind, it is that we must take the long view. We must own and understand the frame of geologic time, and thereby wake up to the fact that we have set in motion forces on the planet that at once are asynchronous with the patterns of evolutionary existence and contrary to life-affirming tendencies. One might argue that this is All Right and according to some, part of the higher "plan." But if this is so, then how do we explain the fact that on a planet where all species strive to further their own existence, just one species – humankind, seems to be on a determinate trajectory to eliminate itself?

37

THE MOUNTAIN SINGS MY SONG

Come to me
My mountain muse,
Spirit me away with your forest fingers,
Caress my back with your beds of soft moss,
Refresh my lips with the bitter taste of lichen,
Quench my thirst with your sweet springs,
So cold
So pure
That my very blood sings,
I long for your promise of balsam breath,
A lover's memory,
An untold death,
For those who have passed can see through
    your eyes,
Feel your age and know your wisdom,
And divine what the future belies,
Yeah that I might know your history!
Hear your powerful hush,

'Cross fell fields and lilies
And tufts of gentle rush,
To see the mist rising as the curtains unfold
The dawn of your greatness and our story
untold.

❧

I have often wondered while climbing in far and distant lands how many others have traveled where I have stood. Only once, in a roadless and remote part of the largest desert in North America, did I believe that I was the first person ever to visit this particular site. Otherwise, I have been mostly certain that others have walked where I have been. What stories did they have to tell? And if the mountains they were traveling on could listen and relate their tales, what stories would the mountains tell? These "traces" of others passing a particular spot exist beyond time, beyond normal waking reality, yet I believe they are likely accessible in some way. Various cultures have talked of being able to access these memories, these events in both "dream time" and waking time. If the history of a place can carry the 'echoes' of visitors gone by, wouldn't it be in our best interest to tread carefully upon the Earth and leave a trace we can be proud of?

38

THOREAUVIAN PRAYER

If in "Wildness is the preservation of the world,"
Then 'In Mountains is the Preservation of the Spirit.'

Stone cold
Giver of life,
Bring forth your power
Of forgiveness,
Warm our hearts
With your icy fire,
Yield softly the trodden feet
Of your verdant green attire,
Shed your tears from
Some forgotten age, and
Cast your life blood
Upon the Earthly stage.

~

The first time I spent the night upon Mount Monadnock in southern New Hampshire in the exact spot where Henry David Thoreau was reputed to have spent the night in 1858, I felt a kinship to the raw experience of living on high without great comfort. This particular night, not unlike what Thoreau recorded in his journal, was "damp and filled with a nasty air." It was October, and exactly 120 years after he had camped in this spot. Because Mount Monadnock, Red Hill, Mount Washington and other mountains had been Thoreau's inspiration if not salvation, I sensed then as I do now a certain kinship for his understanding of how important such wild places are for the human spirit.

39

ONCE UPON A MIDNIGHT SUN

Once upon a midnight sun
A dream of lofty places,
Of icy crags
And heather moor
And silver spiders' laces.

The light had cast
A shadow fast
Upon rock and rush and ripple,
And gathered moss
Between the floss
Of sedge and grass and stipple.

The scape was I,
And I the scape,
In truth my heart believing,
That the mind found fair,
Without despair,

A reflection of its own conceiving.

All beauty within,
Has created without,
A scene of infinite tranquility,
To my spirits I declare,
May this be my lair
Of rest and eternal civility.

$\sim$

I have had only a few reoccurring dreams in my life, one of which returns me each time to a scene in Alaska, not unlike the place on Heney Ridge I wrote about in 'A Mountain At-one-ment.' I travel there, flying across a broad glacial valley with verdant fell fields and braided streams, avalanche chutes and thick glacial shoulders among craggy peaks. There is no particular pattern to this dream other than the soaring flight, as if I am coming home to check on things. There are no signs of people in this wilderness landscape, and I wander there freely as an eagle would, unperturbed by the machinations of civilization. It is here that I would like to rest someday.

A NEW DAWNING

There is then this:
Golden rays of sunlight
Upon a brilliant mountainside cloaked in
     hope,
Breathing in the crystal blue sky,
Water flowing somewhere in the distance by,
Washing the debris of my mind
Down, down, down
Breaking down the bits of misunderstanding
Into clear channels of relief,
Riffle laughter,
Deep pools of tranquility,
I plunge into the depths of life without grief.

I wonder sometimes why it took so long.
How could I let myself feel so much despair?
That I would not want anyone else to tarry
     there?

Why should I release the bull, the boar, the
   angry bear
And suffer the loss of not knowing where
I stand,
There, and now less the presumptive air,
Of fear, loss, and a hollow stare.
This tale I bid good riddance then,
And take my life 'ere back again,
Knowing well the power I've owned and won,
Lies not in what I've seen or done,
But in the word of kindness within,
And love that vanquishes hate and sin,
For mine is naught but light and grace,
As witness I have become this very place,
Undaunted, connected, calm, and at peace,
All fear and loathing and loss I release.

～

I offer up the message of this poem as an alternative to alcohol, drugs, and therapy. The power of healing in nature, whether on a mountain or in some other wild and natural place, has been known and practiced for centuries. The very occupational path I have been on for some fifty years is borne of this truth. By the grace of many an outdoor place, I have witnessed firsthand the healing power of the Earth. For most it may appear as some unbegotten falsehood, some fanciful dream of modern day contrivances attached to some retail idolatry. Yet for all who have experienced such peace and tranquility at the hands of nature, it has and always shall have the power to transform pain and suffering into hope and inspiration.

41

THE MOUNTAIN EVER RISES

Crossing Higher Ground
Becomes
A metaphor for what was lost
And now is found,
Balance and swiftness on high,
An unfolding of wings unbound.
The path seeks the pathfinder,
The forest sheds the tree,
I relinquish all cares inside
And greet eternity.

~

Crossing higher ground connects us with our own spirit by connecting us with the spirit of place. Mountains are indeed a metaphor for life, and offer an honorable path of truth for those who seek it. In the presence of greatness, particularly those places that are beyond comprehensible time, one can regain a sense of self that transcends the fundamental morass of the human collective. At a time when the joy and inspiration of each human spirit is needed more than ever, the honorable path of ascending a mountain can offer the traveler a greater sense of self, elevated hope, and eternal happiness.

EPILOGUE

The paths of climbing a mountain are many. Each step, each pitch, and each leg of the journey is different for everyone. Whereas "the mountains rise to meet us," we can only succeed if we rise to meet them as well.

This short collection of poems was meant to reveal the common themes of a climber, as told through the eyes of one mountaineer. It may resonate with those readers who have suffered the same fate of being drawn to a mountain life, with those who have felt the irresistible urge to 'climb on,' or with those who have sensed the power of survival at the hands of certain death.

The mountain has and always will be a metaphor for life. The struggles we face growing up, learning who we are, testing our skills against the world—all of these things can be experienced by climbing mountains. The four stages of a climb are not unlike the four stages of life—the 'approach' of our youth, the 'ascent' of our early adulthood, the 'traverse' of gaining wisdom through our middle years, and the 'summit cone' of our senior years.

For many this will be the natural progression of the span of one's life. For others, it will be an oft and repeated process through every part of life, whether young or old. Regardless of the timing or sequence of such things, the lessons of the climb are irrefutably present:

- That we share the world with others deserving of our care
- That we often face what may appear to be insurmountable struggles, and yet have the capacity to persevere
- That we stand a better chance of success if we train well for our journey, understand our limitations, and remain calm in the face of adversity
- That what may appear to be an 'easy ride' can actually be beset with pitfalls that will test us and make us stronger and wiser
- That a "rate determining step," regardless of when and where it appears, will require our greatest skill, our greatest attention, and our greatest humility in order to survive; and
- That the success of achieving the summit is only as great as our understanding of the lessons we have learned along the way and our ability to share them with others

Such are the mental musings of one traveler, one climber on a path of his choosing, wishing only to better understand what crossing higher ground means before taking that one final path we all must take one day.

Crossing Higher Ground
Poetry from The Mountaintops

~

Thank You For Reading

As the author of this book, I appreciate you purchasing and reading my poetry. I hope you enjoyed the journey into the mountaintops as much as I did.

I would be grateful if you would leave a book review either with your favorite book distributor or with Amazon.

Please go to my book page to leave your review.

Thank you,

Rick Van de Poll

Ecosystem Management Consultants of New England

ABOUT THE AUTHOR

Dr. Van de Poll continues to put pen to poem as an experienced mountaineer and climber. This is his second book of poetry, which follows *Crossing Paths, A Poetic Journey in 45 Days*. He comes to the field of writing about mountains with a substantial roster of mountain-climbing ascents across Central and North America and Europe, beginning with a five-month trek of the Appalachian Trail in 1973. From the knowledge he has gained in high places, Rick has taught ccology and environmental science at the undergraduate and graduate level for over thirty years. As an environmental consultant, he has worked in all parts of North America and selected locales in Mexico and Italy. He has undertaken and completed comprehensive ecological inventories of over 300,000 acres in 103 towns in New Hampshire, Vermont, Maine, Massachusetts, and New York. He is the principal of Ecosystem Management Consultants and can be reached at **www.rickvandepoll.com**.

ACKNOWLEDGMENTS

There have been a number of mentors along the path of my life as a mountaineer that deserve my recognition. First and foremost, I would like to thank Dr. Willi Unsoeld who, two years after his historic first ascent of the West Ridge of Mount Everest, led the Encounter Program at Phillips Andover Academy and convinced my brother and I to go out and buy a rope. That rope saved us from many a fall throughout high school and during my years at Evergreen State, where Willi once again led us budding mountaineers up mountains and down throughout the Pacific Northwest. Elsewhere in this poetic anthology I recognize Willi's Everest cohorts, Jim Whittaker and Nawang Gombu, who helped guide me up and down Mount Rainier a couple times. Along the mountaineering path many other hardy souls provided company and encouragement, especially Rob Janett on Popocateptl, to who I owe a great deal of gratitude. Lastly, I would like to honor my wife for ensuring that these humble reflections on my past avocation didn't get lost in obscurity.

ALSO BY RICK VAN DE POLL

Crossing Paths: A Poetic Journey in 45 Days

https://amazon.com/dp/B076H7NYBF

Crossing Higher Ground: Poetry from the Mountaintops

∼

**To receive notification when more books
are published , please go to:**

https://rickvandepoll.com/books

∼

You can find my books on Amazon:

https://amazon.com/author/rickvandepoll

www.ingramcontent.com/pod-product-compliance
Lightning Source LLC
Chambersburg PA
CBHW020257030426
42336CB00010B/815